Responses to 'The Reality of Rape'

Reading Jenny's book made me realise I'm not an awful person. I'm a person who was raped and my body reacted by falling apart.
Elizabeth Stewart

Jenny's book is a well written, powerful plea for justice for rape victims.
Suzan, Survivor

'The Reality of Rape' is an extraordinary book. It explores clearly the not very well researched reactions to rape – dissociation, loss of memory and delayed shock. The story does that in an accessible way, making this book essential reading for those who have experienced rape and those who want to reach out and support survivors. Other rape victims will see that it is eventually possible to get on the road to recovery. It's a slow process and we need support and Jenny's story tells us of her journey through trauma. It is a book of hope, courage, anger and love. I can't recommend it more highly. It's a gem of a book.

Dr Sue Atkinson, author of 'Struggling to forgive'

We all know someone who has been raped. This brave and honest book can help us to understand the reality of rape so we can support victim/survivors of this horrendous yet common crime. Jenny writes about a dark topic but despite this, there is so much love, warmth and humanity in this unforgettable memoir.

Nicole, Survivor

This book is about unmeasurable courage. It is a book about the absolute physical cruelty of rape but it is also about the abuse of power, the silencing of the soul and how the predator (and others who colluded with him) attempted to shift their shame onto their victim within a powerful organisation, the NHS. Through the long journey towards recovery it is one woman's story to stand with dignity, and I salute her beautiful bravery.

Helen, Survivor

This powerful book highlights how some abuse their powerful positions to heinously take what is not theirs, for that is what sexual assault is, with no thoughts of the lifelong shattering effects on their victim. Jenny skilfully highlights the very real barriers, still around in the 21st Century towards justice for those who have experienced sexual assault. Until we as a society wake up to this, women, children and some men are not safe. And to Jenny, I say, I am so sorry that a man, who should have cherished you, hurt you in this way. Thank you for the privilege of hearing your story.

Ann Vaughan, Survivor

I found Jenny's heart-breaking story powerful and moving. It is very brave that Jenny was able to share what happened to her and everyone needs to read about the reality of rape and the trauma it causes to the victims. Even though, I was not surprised by the lack of help from professionals or the gruelling process which victims go through, I strongly believe that people need to read Jenny's account, and hopefully develop empathy to stop victim blaming. I am not a survivor myself but have worked for a number of years with vulnerable young women. Sadly, a lot of their stories echo Jenny's.

Jessica Morales

Jenny's memoir is a brutally honest and brave account which amongst many things proves that people who are fortunate enough not to have experienced rape can have no possible idea of the impact it has on someone's life. If they did, the systems would be better organised with attention paid to important details. I am shocked at how many cases are reported and even more so to find out that this is fewer than

20% of the total cases. It's too easy to get away with doing this to people and something needs to change.
Lisa Atkinson

Wow! This book is an easy read but so real it both inspires and challenges. Jenny is incredibly brave writing with such truth and clarity. Thank you.
A survivor in Liverpool.

Jenny Cooke's memoir of her life across 35 years after being raped is remarkable. Her story carries highly insightful accounts of her mental pain, often accentuated by dismissive or wildly inappropriate responses to her seeking help. Joy is apparent, too – but it is fragile and commonly short-lived.

This compelling and thoughtful narrative deserves the widest possible readership. It is a timely shout for compassion and far better understanding towards the victims of such hidden violence.
Professor Richard Vincent at Brighton and Sussex Medical School.

I've just finished Jenny's account of her rape and feel so angry for her with the dreadful way it was handled - or not handled. Why, oh why is it always the woman who carries the shame and the blame? It's of course not just in our culture. As far as I know, it's hard-wired into all societies.

I would recommend that her account be read

widely. It's a raw and real and uncomfortable read but these truths need to be brought into the open.

At least we can begin to do this openly in our society, and bring the whole issue of rape to be seen for the terrible, lifelong damage it wreaks on the victims and their families

Meriel Vincent.

THE REALITY OF RAPE

The Reality of Rape

JENNY COOKE

Survivors Voices Press

This book is dedicated to the late Eileen Steinitz, counsellor and friend

Chapter 1

Someone asked me the question, what breaks your heart? This was my answer. The centuries of suffering of women break my heart. The way a man can treat a woman breaks my heart. The inequality between men and women breaks my heart. The suffering of women at the hands of manipulative men breaks my heart. The suffering of children who grow into traumatised adults breaks my heart. The pain of sexual violence shatters my heart into splinters of pain. I am in agony from the splinters piercing my being, my body, my soul.

In the year to the end of 2023, 68,387 cases of rape were recorded by police forces in England and Wales. Charges were brought in just 1,778 cases. Fewer than 3 in 100 rapes recorded resulted in a charge that same year let alone a conviction. The legal system is failing women with a shocking lack of convictions.

Rape is often not reported because of the shame the victim feels and also because the victim does not believe they will receive justice. Of those that do report rape many say they feel re-traumatised by the process. Rape is an intimate, heinous crime and has a lifelong impact on the victim-survivor. It can take years of therapy to begin to shed the shame that results from it. The shame should lie with the perpetrator not the victim. We live in a society where victim blaming is all too common.

This is my story of living with the impact of rape. There is no gentle way to write about it. There is no way to soften the edges. Even after all these years it still impacts me. I was 21 when I was raped and I am now 58 so that's 37 years ago. 37 years is a long time to live with the devastation of rape. There have been times when I wished I could go to sleep and never wake up, when living felt just too hard and feelings of revulsion were too great. However, I do still wake up each day and make it through till night. I am thankful that I have survived and have been here to witness my children grow into wonderful, caring adults.

For a really long time I couldn't remember exactly what happened in 1986 on New Year's Eve. I had carried on with life as normal and it wasn't until I was 37 that parts of that night came back into my awareness in the most awful way.

There was a time when I didn't know what a flashback was. I didn't know that I was living in such blissful ignorance. The full horror of my experience was yet to be revealed to me. I was walking around with a ticking bomb ready to shatter the very core of my being. I once read that trauma was like a bomb going off underwater but that means the water would cushion the shock. I had no cushion when the bomb exploded. The pain was absolute.

Sixteen years after the rape, when I was 37, I enrolled on a bereavement visitor training course. It seemed like a good idea. I'd done a lot of terminal care when I was district nursing and always felt there was a lack of support for the family after the death. Each week I went along to the course and started to feel more and more uneasy. I would wake in the night with a feeling of deep apprehension. We spent time looking at the intense emotions that accompany grief. We looked at a variety of different types of losses. We were given a piece of paper with different losses written all over it and there right at the bottom of the page was a small, four lettered word, rape. Still, I didn't know if that word had anything to do with me but it stood out.

I got to the end of the course and the trainer, Eileen, spent some time talking to each of us individually. I welled up when I spoke to her and explained that I'd left my work as a District Nurse after being stressed and developing a needle phobia. It had been a hugely difficult decision to leave the profession I loved but

I couldn't seem to get past the needle phobia and as a nurse I needed to be able to give injections. I saw a psychologist a few times but didn't really connect with him and his strategies for managing the needle phobia didn't help. My children were young and I decided to take a career break. We had no family nearby and my husband Pete worked long hours. Eileen suggested that I come along for a few counselling sessions as she was a counsellor as well as trainer. I was so naïve. I had no idea of the explosion that was to come.

It was December when I went for my first counselling session. I talked about work stress and made another appointment for the next week. By the second session I said I'd had an experience that might be called date rape now but I wasn't sure. I was very tentative. In the sixteen years since it happened, I had not used the word rape. I had not named it or been able to speak about it. I didn't want the word to belong to me. By not saying it meant that it was less real. I'll always remember Eileen's words as she said 'rape is rape' and offered that I could still report it if I wanted to. At that time, I had no desire to report it. I walked out of the counselling room feeling shell shocked but had no time to dwell on it as it was time to pick up my children from school.

What happened after this was worse than anything I could ever have imagined. It was Christmas time and I almost completely stopped sleeping. Every night as

I was at that moment between waking and sleeping, I was hit by a physical jolt and then re-living the night I was raped. It was like it was actually happening and my body would contract with the force of him. Night after night I re-lived the awful sensations. New things came into my awareness that I had no previous recollection of. I felt sick and overcome with revulsion. I lost my appetite. I was terrified and thought I was losing my mind. I was sure I must be mad and if I told a doctor what was happening, I would be sectioned. I would lose my children if anyone knew how mad I was.

Eventually I managed to convey something of how bad I was feeling to a close friend. She sensibly suggested that I contact my counsellor even though it was during the Christmas break. Eileen calmly explained that I was experiencing trauma and brought forward my appointment. I remember walking up the road to see her and treading really carefully. If I moved carefully and slowly, I might not trigger the pain. I can still see the shoes I was wearing. My feet were changed. My world was irrevocably changed. I felt the full horror of the flashbacks and didn't know how I was going to survive. The need to care for my children was my motivation for getting through each day. I was so thankful to have my children and Pete to help me connect with the present when the past was so overwhelming and intrusive.

Chapter 2

1986

When I was growing up, I thought that 21 sounded like a magical age where you became truly grown up. My mother had a small tan coloured leather suitcase with a silk lining that had been a twenty-first birthday present and it seemed to hold an element of glamour. I aspired to some of that glamour. Just after my twenty-first birthday I was about to qualify as a staff nurse and change from my student nurse's pale blue uniform to a bright white uniform. I had no idea that very soon I would feel unworthy of the colour white, a virginal colour. I would spend years feeling too dirty and spoilt to want to wear it. I would also spend years feeling afraid of white coats. Even now as I write, I feel an apprehension at telling my story. Putting it into words makes the experience more real and for a long time the rape wasn't real to me.

To write about it is to acknowledge the reality of rape. I hate the word and yet it is part of who I am, I am a woman who has experienced rape. When it happened, I had no words for the experience.

So here goes, deep breath, this is my story. On New Year's Eve I was excited to be going out to a party. I wore a navy-blue dress with orange stripes and sheer navy tights. I had new shoes. They were black suede and I felt glamorous in them. The party was in the common room of the hospital where I lived and worked. It was hot and crowded and I was foolish enough to be drinking the punch, who knew what was in it? I'd been out a couple of times with someone called John. He was a doctor who I worked with in the run up to the Christmas period and he was with me at the party. Someone had said to me 'I hear you're seeing a dangerous man' as a sort of throw away comment and I didn't ask them to elaborate. What did they know about him that I didn't? I still wonder about it, what else had he done and why was I so naïve as to miss any warning signals? Had he raped other nurses?

The night moved on and sometime after midnight we went back to my room. Now call me stupid but I really did not know what was going to happen. I was a young 21. I'd had boyfriends but I was a good Catholic girl and I hadn't had sex. I was saving myself for the one. I'm aware that it sounds faintly ridiculous now but that was how I thought back then.

I will never know exactly what happened that night. For years I could only remember reaching my room door and nothing else. When it came back into my awareness, sixteen years later, I remembered fragments. I know I felt a weight on top of me. I know that I was pinned against the wall by my bed. I know that eventually he slept and I was trapped but most of all I know that I was bleeding a lot. I was bleeding and terrified to move. I didn't want to disturb him in case he started again. Time ceased to exist. Eventually I heard birds singing and thought it must be nearly morning. I inched my way out of the bed and went to the toilet down the corridor. This was the first of many visits to the toilet and I was so afraid of anyone seeing the blood. I dripped onto the toilet floor and was methodical in my cleaning up. No one must know.

John left to go to work, he was on-call. I don't remember speaking to him as he left. Thus began the longest day. I wanted to die. I thought about taking an overdose but didn't have enough tablets. What could be worse than overdosing and failing to succeed? I'd cared for patients who had taken overdoses and ended up with liver or kidney damage and I didn't want to be one of them. But what would I do? The bleeding got worse and worse and went on and on. I was upset about my quilt cover as it was very blood stained. It had been a twenty-first birthday present and was a lovely paisley pattern. It was ruined. I watched the hours passing by on my clock radio.

I reached the point where I realised that if I didn't do something I would die alone in my room from the bleeding. I went to a friend and told her I thought I'd had sex and I was bleeding a lot. We then had this terrible dilemma about what to do. I couldn't go to the Accident and Emergency Unit in the hospital where we worked because I would know too many people but where could I go? We got a taxi to another hospital a few miles away. I was terrified getting into the taxi as I didn't want to make a mess of the seats. My friend put something under me to save the seat.

The next few hours were appalling. I lay on a trolley with a frayed old blanket over me. I remember being cold. Staff asked me who did this and I called him my boyfriend. They asked where he was and I said he was working, he was a doctor, he was on-call. After that it went silent. No one said what's happened to you isn't right or suggested that I could report it to the police. I can only assume that they were protecting their own, no point in reporting a doctor. Because I was met with silence, I became silent and stayed that way for the next sixteen years. I needed to go to theatre to be stitched as they thought it would be better for me under anaesthetic.

Before I went to theatre I was taken to a ward. I remember a nurse asking me about bruises on my legs. I lied and said it was busy on the ward I worked on and I was always bumping into things. She accepted what I said although the bruising was clearly finger marks. Then she asked me for a urine sample. I said I couldn't give her one as I was bleeding too heavily but she insisted. I still remember her look of shock when she saw a jug of thick blood. I was wheeled along the corridor to the operating theatre. Never has anyone been so relieved to be anaesthetised. I really, really didn't want to wake up. I came to back on the ward and it was night time. The only lights came from a Christmas tree. I felt the burning misery of those lights and wished I were dead. For years and years, I have hated Christmas tree lights.

Afterwards I tried to carry on with life as if it hadn't happened. I was unaware that it was influencing every part of my life. Looking back, I think I was so traumatised that the only way I could cope was by blocking the memories. How could I go back and live in the room where I was raped if the rape was in the front of my mind the whole time?

I guess the big question is why didn't I tell anyone what had happened to me? I wasn't given the opportunity to speak about my experience when I was in the hospital and even if I had been encouraged to speak out, I didn't have the words for the experience.

I really didn't understand what I'd been through. I felt a huge amount of confusion. I knew that I had bled a lot and it was easier to think that there must have been something physically wrong with me rather than admit that what this man had done was wrong. It was so easy to believe that it was my fault because I had let him into my room. I had to be to blame. If he was to blame it would make my world too unpredictable. It would mean that anyone was capable of attacking me at any time and I couldn't comprehend that.

I remember one day about five weeks after it happened when I was out for a walk and there was blue sky and sunshine. It was the first time that I thought thank God, I'm alive.

My body complained about carrying on as normal and I kept being ill. I got laryngitis and lost my voice completely. Then I caught chicken pox from a patient who has shingles. My parents didn't want me to come home in case they caught shingles so I isolated in my room in the nurses' home, the same room that I'd been raped in. I felt itchy and low and miserable. Once I recovered from chicken pox, I continued to feel unwell. I had a constant sore throat and swollen glands in my neck. One of the doctors who I worked with said maybe I have glandular fever. He did a blood test for me and late one evening I was sorting through patients' blood test results when I came across my own result. It confirmed that I have glandular fever.

I wrote in my diary saying 'I don't want sick time so I think I'll carry on working if I'm O.K. I'm fed up. I'd like to trade my body in for a new one!'

One of the effects of being raped was that I felt completely separate from my body. It was as if my head and my body were not connected and it was only years later when I was in therapy that I began to address this feeling of detachment. Also, if I took time off work it would give me time to think and I didn't want that.

Chapter 3

1992, 5 years after the rape

I start the year feeling happy. I spent time visiting my boyfriend, Pete's family in Ireland over the Christmas break and had an amazing time. He would later become my husband. I came back to work feeling good. I'd qualified the previous year as a District Nurse and I loved the work. I was proud to wear the royal blue uniform of a District Nursing Sister and manage my own caseload.

Things were about to change. At the end of January, I went on a bike ride and felt light headed and faint. A few days later I went to France with friends. I stood on the beach in a freezing wind and thought what if I'm pregnant? Another few days and my period was late. I did a pregnancy test and it was positive. Within a few more days I started being sick every day and feeling nauseous the whole time. Pete was understanding and we decided to move in together and get engaged.

I couldn't hide my pregnancy because I was so sick. I refused to take any time off work and drove to see patients with a plastic bag in the car in case I was sick. I remember standing on doorsteps retching. I was last out of the clinic in the mornings as I was in the toilet throwing up. People kept reassuring me that by the time I was 12 weeks pregnant I would stop being sick, then by 14 weeks and then by 16 weeks but it didn't stop. I had a burst blood vessel in my eye from retching. I lost weight almost instantly. My bump started to grow but I was like a stick insect with skinny arms and legs.

I cried every single day of my pregnancy. It's only more recently that we are beginning to recognise ante-natal depression as well as post-natal depression. I remember one midwife asking me about the sickness and then asking if I had any previous difficult experiences. It didn't for one moment enter my head that I had been violently raped 5 years previously. It just wasn't in my awareness. I think that denial served a purpose. It helped to keep me safe. After all, how could I put myself in the hands of the medical profession that had failed to take adequate care of me and trust that my baby would be safely delivered?

I prepare to tell my parents that I am pregnant. Pete wants to come with me but I refuse to let him. It feels like I should shoulder that responsibility. I visit my parents and want to talk to them, but this isn't easy. I start with 'could we turn the television off? I'd like to talk to you.' Dad then says that he is watching Last of the Summer Wine! I try again and we manage to turn the TV off. I tell them that I'm getting engaged and that I'm pregnant and then burst into tears. Mum wants to know why I'm crying. 'That's wonderful news' she says. That's when I realise, she hasn't heard the part about me being pregnant. I have to summon up my courage, raise my voice and tell her again that I'm pregnant. Both parents go quiet and stay that way. They never openly show their disapproval but during the next few months Mum makes little barbed comments, 'they always say it's the quiet ones you have to watch!'

A work colleague is on maternity leave and a few of us go to visit her and the new baby one lunchtime. I am shocked to see a real live baby - shocked and horrified. Am I really going to have one of these? I do not know what to do with a new baby. The ante-natal classes prepare me for the labour and delivery but no one says anything much about what to do with the baby once it has safely arrived. For years afterwards colleagues remind me of how scared I looked that day.

We move into our new house just three weeks before my due date. The baby is lying with its spine against mine and I have excruciating sciatica. It's really hard moving house while I am in so much pain. Thankfully, the baby moves to a better position before I go into labour. Pete helps as much as he can with unpacking boxes but he is working long hours and most of the unpacking falls to me as I am now on maternity leave. I continue to be sick every day and it is so uncomfortable throwing up with a big bump. At ante-natal classes we are told that one of the signs of the start of labour can be sickness. This isn't really helpful for me; how will I know the difference between pregnancy sickness and the start of labour?

I make friends with women from my ante-natal group. One of them invites us for lunch when her baby is about two weeks old. I feel very tired and have a low crampy back pain all day. The friend who invites us for lunch is glowing with love for her baby and wants to show us a video of the birth. The video focuses on her and then moves to the clock on the wall and we see how she endures hours of labour. I feel very emotional watching the delivery and can't sleep that night. I am ten days overdue and am in the early stages of labour. The next day I have a sense of calm and I set about making bread. It seems like the most natural thing in the world to bake bread and I love the smell of it. Maybe this is what's meant by nesting.

I want to stay upright to try and help labour get established. I do loads of ironing. I have another sleepless night. The next day is Saturday and I go for a walk in the park next to our house. It's October and it feels wonderful to be out in the Autumn air. My contractions are getting stronger and I stop walking and hold onto Pete and breathe in the fresh air. I feel calm and want to stay at home for as long as I can. After the third sleepless night my contractions start to get closer together. Late on Sunday afternoon we call the hospital and prepare to go in, but the car won't start. We call a taxi but I don't tell them I'm in labour in case they won't take us. I breathe through the contractions and want to laugh when the taxi driver asks what department we want.

Our son, Jack, is born at 11.15pm and I am overjoyed. I cannot believe how beautiful and perfect he is and I feel happier than I have ever felt. That night I am so elated that I don't sleep. I spend a magical night looking through the side of the clear plastic cot at Jack. My bed is by a window and I look out at the night sky and thank God for the miracle of new life.

The next day I feel really odd. I think I might faint and have to sit down. The nurse says in an accusing tone that I don't look like I'm going to faint, my colour is good. I feel as if I've been told off. By lunchtime I have a migraine that starts with tingling in my fingers and visual disturbance before the pain hits. It's only years later that I begin to make sense of what was happening that morning. I think that on a subconscious level I was working really hard to make sure the rape didn't come back to me. Giving birth is such a vulnerable time and I think the trauma was very close to the surface. There were so many things that could have triggered memories of the rape. I was in the same hospital as when I was raped in my room in the nurses' home at the back of the hospital. Going anywhere near a hospital and being in contact with medical professionals were things that I really struggled with later on after the rape came back into my consciousness. I'm so thankful that it stayed out of my awareness when my son Jack was born and I was able to experience the absolute joy of new life without horrific memories intruding.

Chapter 4

2007, twenty years after the rape

It's the end of January 2007. I feel woolly and off balance and have a cold. I had a dream. I dreamt I was in the middle of a field. I was lying on a hospital trolley in a flimsy tent and it was blowing open in the breeze. There were people outside, wandering around. A woman appeared at the end of the trolley to examine me. I woke up feeling horribly exposed.

Our cat's come home. I'd missed her. She's been gone for days on end. I came across a picture of her as a kitten yesterday and missed her some more. She's mine. I've looked after her, loved her and now someone else is feeding her. This morning she walked sheepishly up the garden path. She smells of perfume. I feel betrayed, she's a two-timing, fickle cat. But I forgive her. She can keep secrets and doesn't answer back.

I'm feeling quite good by mid-February. It's a relief to get past Christmas and New Year when there are so many reminders of what happened to me. I'm in the second year of my counselling training and enjoying it. I have two placements and I'm keen to get my 200 hours of client work that I need for my BA in Person-Centred counselling. I also do some part-time work running a group for new mothers who need extra support and it's a space for them to meet others with similar age babies and share experiences. In addition to this I work for a small local charity as a Parent Mentor where I work with parents who often have complex needs.

I've reached the stage where my children are beginning to be a bit more independent. My son, Jack is 15 and my daughters, Rachel and Annie, are 12 and 9 which means I'm still tied to the school run for Annie. It is a source of joy that the older two can now travel independently to school. The downside is that they are all at different schools and I have to deal with three different term dates as they never seem to co-ordinate the start and end of term. Pete continues to work long hours and so I struggle to get time to study. I usually carve out time to work on essays in the evening and I find it immensely satisfying when I start to get good grades.

In February I attend a bereavement conference. One of the workshops was facilitated by someone who worked as a senior nurse in casualty for many years. I so wanted to ask her about what the procedure was in the 1980's if someone presented in need of medical attention following sexual assault. I know that how I was treated doesn't feel right but somehow, I want official confirmation of this. Would the staff have asked about what had happened? Most importantly, would they have suggested it could be reported to the police? Or was it something that they were not really equipped to deal with? I really want to ask those questions and because the workshop facilitator happens to work with another student on my course, I know I could easily get in contact with her. It's so tempting to want to do that.

I gather up my courage and arrange to meet with this retired nurse one afternoon the following week. We meet in a room attached to her church. I feel nervous and it's hard to get started. I give her a brief outline of my experience in hospital after being raped. I tell her that I want to know if I was treated differently because the man who raped me was a doctor. By failing to name my experience as rape or offer that I could report it to the police, were they protecting him? She explains that there were policies in place for dealing with sexual assault when someone comes into A+E. They would have included giving the victim the opportunity to report what had happened to the police. However, she described a culture where it was very much hit and miss as to whether this would happen. Many staff made their own judgements, 'she was drunk' or 'she must have asked for it.' Yes, I was drunk but I didn't ask for it. This confirms what I had thought but it's good to hear it from someone who worked in A+E in 1987.

The next part gets difficult. She decides to preach to me about forgiveness. I would feel so much better if I could forgive the perpetrator. I am speechless. Is this the price I have to pay for the information that I wanted? I tell her that I am working on forgiving myself. On my way home I cry tears of frustration and rage. How dare this woman tell me I should forgive the man who raped me. Has he apologised? No! Then I am unable to contemplate forgiveness. Doubt starts to creep in. Does this make me a bad person because I can't forgive. This woman has added to the burden of guilt and shame that I carry as a survivor of rape.

It's Easter time. I've been through some of the darkest times where I felt overwhelmed with revulsion and disgust at what was done to me. Now I can feel warmth and light. God's love shines around me. I can allow myself to feel it more fully. I feel clean and new.

It is such a relief to feel better but sadly it only lasts for a short time.

I start to have headaches and feel incredibly tired. I gradually feel worse and worse and I am slightly nauseous a lot of the time. My 12 year old daughter, Rachel, complains of feeling dizzy at the bus stop on her way to school. I stop writing in my journal and it's several months before I try to make sense of my experience. During this time, we find out that we are suffering from carbon monoxide poisoning. We are shocked to find that it has been coming from our gas hob which is old and hasn't been burning properly.

It's August when I surface enough to write. I took two months off from my work with clients and families. It was all I could do to look after our family. I quickly lost weight as I had no appetite and continued to feel slightly nauseous. It was the most terrifying time that I have ever experienced. I don't know how to get the feelings of terror across in words. It was beyond words. I guess that goes with trauma. How can I explain what it was like?

Nothing, but nothing felt safe. I was shaken to my core and then some more. Everything was frightening. It didn't matter what I did, where I went or what I looked at, it was all unsafe. As I write this, I start to feel uneasy again. Perhaps trying to explore the trauma was a bad idea. It literally makes me want to get up and run as fast as I can, to run away from the memory of the feelings. So, what frightened me so much? I could just say everyone and everything but it was more specific than that. It was anything sexual. All people became threatening and then it extended to everything around me. Objects became terrifying as I could turn almost anything into something phallic. The thoughts came uninvited and at high-speed leaving me feeling that I was mad, that I was revolting for having such thoughts. Everything was frightening. I'd never experienced anything like this.

As well as fear the pain was indescribable. Was it emotional or physical? I couldn't say. It was all encompassing, all consuming. I was on fire. My whole body hurt. I felt so wicked that I thought I couldn't continue to exist. Then I remembered that this was an old thought. I wanted to 'cease to exist'. Such a gentle way of saying that I wanted to die.

If I thought childbirth was the worst pain that I would have to endure then I was wrong. This was relentless and left me no time to breathe. I was aware of every painful moment and each breath burnt. There was no relief and it didn't matter how hard I tried to explain to people that I felt mad, no-one believed me. But I felt so crazy, so frightened. I felt more and more distant from the world as it continued to view me as sane. The tension between this outer image and what I felt inside was huge. I struggled to eat or sleep as the tension grew. I worry that I won't be able to look after our children but maintaining their routines helps me. Knowing that they need me is what pushes me to put one foot in front of the other.

Eventually I find proof that I am mad. My doctor refers me to a psychiatrist. It's my worst fear, a nightmare come true. I keep thinking that any moment now I'll wake up and there's been a mistake, this is meant to be someone else, not me!

I go to see the psychiatrist. Pete comes with me. He knows that I was raped when I was 21 and has tried to support me as much as possible. He has found it hard to witness my distress but he's remained a calming presence. My legs will hardly carry me. I am about to combust with fear. Then I meet a young psychiatrist. He looks like someone from a bad comedy sketch. He has a long white face and asks me a series of irrelevant questions. What results did I get in my A levels? Does he want to know how intelligent I am or is he testing my memory? I can remember some things. We get to the more relevant bits. When was my first sexual experience.? I watch him squirm as I answer, when I was raped by a doctor when I was 21. Was any legal action taken? No, they didn't offer the opportunity to report it when I went to Casualty, he was a doctor! Would I like to see a female psychiatrist next time? Yes, probably. After due consideration he concludes that I am not psychotic. I have PTSD. Go away and take the anti-depressants.

Chapter 5

December 2007, twenty years after the rape

I want to lie down and die, to curl up somewhere quiet and never wake up. Then I'm confused, a thought cuts in, that's a dreadful thing to think. I can't be thinking like that. It's wrong, it's wicked. Life is sacred. But it hurts so much to be alive. I look at all the reminders of Christmas and am submerged with pain. Does it start from the outside or the inside? I've no idea. It's in every part of me. Don't panic, feel the feelings, it might be better than fighting them. So, allow myself to want to go to sleep and never wake up, to cease to exist? Perhaps I could let myself wallow, really wallow in being miserable. Usually, I try to pull myself out of it, pull myself together. Suddenly I want to wallow. I want to make a huge, big noisy fuss, why should I be o.k. when there are so many things reminding me of what happened? I'm tired of being polite, being pleasant, bringing out my smile.

Time moves on. I go to Annie's school concert. She is 9 years old and very excited that I am coming to see her perform. I am miserably aware of the Christmas lights around the back of the stage. And then there's Annie. She's beautiful, she's smiling. She wears red and has stripes painted on her cheeks. Her blond hair shines out of the top of her head band. She's part of an Indian tribe. She smiles, she sings, she has rhythm, she's having the best ever time after all that practise of her one line. She sees me in the dark. I see her. I'm at the back of the hall, there are crowds of people between us but we are connected. We can't believe it. We keep checking it out, I smile, she smiles, we smile. It's as if the path between us is illuminated. I've never experienced anything like it. I'm fascinated, we keep checking that it's real, keep smiling each other's smile. It's happened. I am still capable of feeling joy.

The joy injects some energy through me. I have more energy to understand the Christmas tree and its burning pain. It's not only burning pain or wanting to curl up and die. It's furious, raging anger with what happened on that night, that day in hospital, that foolish, blind, doctor. No-one questioned anything, no-one made any acknowledgement of what had happened.

A few weeks later I was in a coffee shop and picked up a copy of the Guardian newspaper. There is a two-page spread about one woman's personal journey over a period of months from when she reported rape to when the crown prosecution service decided not to bring it any further. It was a very moving account of what she went through in that time, including flashbacks and panic attacks. By the end of it I was welling up in the coffee shop. Afterwards I decided I had to read the article again and queued up for ages to buy the paper. Not only that, I felt moved to respond with a letter to thank the Guardian for Beth Ellis's story.

Late the next evening I e-mailed my letter to the Guardian. I'd spent my therapy session in the morning in floods of tears because I was back to feeling disgusting and revolting and really disheartened by this. But I felt much better after writing my letter. The next morning, I eagerly checked my e-mails and found an automated response from the paper. Then in the afternoon Annie answered the phone and told me it was someone important. It was the letters editor telling me that my letter would be published in full with no changes the next day. I was so excited and it was difficult because I couldn't tell the children what I was excited about. I phoned my sister and let her know that my letter would be published in the Guardian newspaper.

The next morning my daughter Rachel was unwell so we went to the Doctors and then onto the supermarket to collect her prescription. I left her reading magazines while I tore open the Guardian and found the letters page. There's nothing like seeing something you've written in print in a national paper. The one thing that I'd thought long and hard about was putting my name to it. In the end I decided that it was more sensible not to. I was working as a trainee counsellor and Parent Mentor. How would I feel if one of my clients or parents I supported read it? Or what if my own parents read it? I had never felt able to tell them about my experience. I was sad not to put my name because it feeds into the silence and shame around rape but I couldn't really see a way around it.

The other thing that it brought up for me was who could I tell or show the letter to? It was actually quite limited. If it were on any other subject, I would want to tell everyone but this is different. As my counsellor said it would be easier to say I'd just come out of prison!

Here is my letter. It is captioned "Time we all took a stand against rape"

Thank-you for giving Beth Ellis a voice (One woman's ordeal, January 14). I was raped by someone I trusted. Like Beth, I have experienced panic attacks and horrific flashbacks. I don't have her courage to report the rape and also there seems to be little to be gained from doing so. I often feel isolated and furious with a society that isn't able to talk about rape. It's one of the last taboos. It compounds the feeling that I had when it happened. I wasn't equipped with the language to talk about it and believed that it was hugely shameful. Nancy Raine writes: "Rape has long been considered a crime so unspeakable, so shameful to its victims, that they are rendered mute and cloaked in protective anonymity". She adds "The victims of rape must carry their memories with them for the rest of their lives. They must not also carry the burden of silence and shame." Thank you, Beth, for breaking that silence.

Chapter 6

2008, twenty-one years after the rape

As part of my work with families I am required to attend child protection training. On this particular course the training is run by an ex-police officer called Bruce. Bruce is very engaging and really brings the subject alive. During the morning, he talks about historic cases of child abuse and how it has been possible to prosecute perpetrators many years after the event. As I listen, I feel something shift inside me. If it was possible to prosecute historic cases what did this mean for me. I wasn't a child when I was raped, I was 21 but maybe I could still do something about it. I'd never thought I would want to as I thought the likelihood of it going anywhere was very small.

I wait behind at the end of the training session and talk to Bruce. I give him a quick outline of what happened to me. He is really understanding and says 'I believe you' which feels hugely important. He gives me the name and number of someone in the Sapphire Unit which deals with sexual assault. I make the call that week and things seem to move quickly after I speak with a female police officer. She arranges for me to come in and do a video recorded interview at my local police station the following week. I talk to my counsellor Eileen about it. She wants to know who will go with me. I hadn't given it any thought. I just assumed I would go by myself but maybe it would be better to have someone with me. The only person that feels appropriate is Eileen. I ask her if this is possible and to my great relief, she says she can.

I feel so much that I have to do this. This is what I am ready to do right now. Also, when I look back it's what I've been working towards for a long time almost without being aware of it.

In the end the first meeting isn't quite what I was expecting. There was a change of plan and I had a preliminary chat and will do the video interview in a few days' time. I'm glad of that as the whole experience is a lot to take in.

Eileen and I went together. I drove. We walked up the road after parking and went into the police station. There is a locked door with only one person at a time allowed through to the desk. We waited in this tiny lobby area for about ten minutes with a couple of dodgy looking characters. After a while we noticed a phone on the wall with various departments listed, none of which seemed quite appropriate but I tried one and was told to ring the Sapphire unit on my mobile. My hands were literally shaking at this point and I wanted to run away and forget the whole idea. It was hard waiting. Eventually someone called Emma came and met us and took us around the back to the interview block. I was so immensely glad to have Eileen with me. I don't know how I could possibly have thought that I would be ok going by myself.

We went into an interview room together. Eileen was invited in and allowed to stay with me although this will not be the case when I come back to do the video interview. Emma pointed out the cameras on the ceiling and the microphones on the walls. She asked me to say something about why I was there. It was really hard to get started when I was talking to someone who I had only just met. As soon as I mentioned the word rape she changed from a large notepad to a small notepad and afterwards I was asked to read and sign these notes. On the last page I had to sign immediately after the last word to ensure that nothing could be added later.

Emma then left the room and went to get someone called Simon who specialises in sexual crimes and who was from the safety unit. He introduced himself and was keen to put me at ease and let me know that he was there for me. After a while I began to wonder who he was actually trying to reassure. He said he was there to be hassled. If I have any questions at any time, I can phone either him or Emma. If I'm awake in the middle of the night and think of anything write it down and call him in the morning.

The video interview that I am going to do could be used as part of my evidence if the case goes to court. At the very least the police will be contacting the man who raped me to let him know that an allegation has been made against him. This feels like such an enormous thing to be doing. I find it hard to say his name. Eileen said it was the first time that she'd heard his full name.

At the end Simon said that I could be picked up by someone next week to come into the Police Station. Eileen made me laugh. She said, "what in a marked car!" I opted to make my own way there. As we left, she commented on things that I hadn't really noticed. She was surprised to see so many police vans at the back of the station but why was she surprised? Where else would they keep them? The whole thing was quite surreal. Afterwards I felt so exhausted. We were there for just over an hour but it could have been any length of time. I was incredibly moved by something Eileen said. She was asked who she was in relation to me and she replied counsellor and friend which is exactly what she has been. It was so touching to hear that.

The following week I am awake from about 5am on the day I'm going to do the interview. Again, Eileen comes with me. When we get to the police station, I'm told there may be a problem with doing the interview. I start to feel panicky; I can't go through this build up again. Eventually someone comes and explains that because the rape happened in the neighbouring borough, I should be doing the interview there and not in the borough where I live. However, as I am already here, they finally decide that the interview will go ahead.

Eileen is taken to a room next door to the interview room where she can see in but I can't see her. The interview starts and I am asked so many questions. How far was the bed from the door? How big was the room? What was I wearing? What happened after going into my room. I want so much to give the right answers. I also want them to know what things came into my awareness when I had flashbacks. I explain the content of the flashbacks which include some horrific details. Eventually the questions are over. Eileen comes back into the room and her eyes are red. Another police officer who has been outside with Eileen says that I did really, really well in the interview. I don't know how to feel once it's over. It's one of the hardest things that I have ever done. The police say they will keep me updated on progress with my case.

Not much happens for several weeks and when it does, I am so angry. I want to calm down so I go for a walk to our allotment and pick vegetables. The police have been in touch with John and they have given him my married name. I didn't know this would happen and I feel really apprehensive. He could easily google my name and see where I am currently working. I feel scared that he might contact me.

The police want to confirm that they have the right person and email John asking him to confirm the dates that he worked at the hospital. He doesn't do this and asks the police to call him. Then he isn't available at the time they arrange and his secretary calls to re-arrange. Each time the police call me to keep me updated it is a different police officer. I'm meant to have one named officer but this doesn't happen. I find it really hard speaking to different people. They call at odd moments to check or clarify things. I find myself in a crowded coffee shop talking about something deeply painful. Each phone call is difficult. They are speaking to the man who raped me and this has the effect of making him feel closer. He is only a call away. Also, the police use first names all the time. It all sounds really chummy and friendly. Laura has spoken to John, not Detective Constable X has spoken to Mr Y. I can't bring myself to say his name but I have to hear it repeatedly. Soon it is a solicitor not his secretary that answers calls from the police. John works in the North of England as a consultant neuro-surgeon.

By the end of the Summer, four months after my recorded interview, the police are ready to travel to the North of England and interview John.

Chapter 7

September 08, twenty-one years and eight months after the rape

I managed to meet with someone from victim support. Not easy! I wanted more information about the whole process after reporting a rape to the Sapphire unit. I felt confused and uncertain about everything. I am now on my fourth contact person. Is this standard practice or have I been unlucky? I want to know, what is the norm? Also is it common practice to give my married name to the man who raped me without my permission or at the very least informing me first? Also, what happens next? Maybe Victim Support will be able to answer some of my questions.

I look up the national and local numbers. After some deliberation I decide to call the national number. I have done work with several local voluntary organisations and there is the possibility that I could come across someone I know from my local area. After hanging on for ages listening to music that fades in and out someone answers. I tell her a bit about my circumstances and the information that I am looking for. She is very nice and very sympathetic but tells me that my questions need to be directed to the police. The problem is I want someone from outside the police to inform me about their procedures. When I tell her that I am on my fourth contact person and they gave him my name without consulting me she says I can complain to the head of department at the Sapphire Unit. I don't want to complain. I still need the police to continue with their enquiries. This lady on the phone, somewhere out in the ether, suggests that I phone my local victim support. I find it really difficult talking about this with yet another person with whom I have no connection. It's not the sort of subject that rolls off the tongue easily to an unknown voice. After all it took me 16 years to begin to be able to say the word rape.

I am determined to find out more. I phone my local number. They say they don't really know the answers to my questions but the manager will call me back. She calls back within the hour and again I say what I am looking for, which is information about the whole process of reporting a rape, a historical case, to the police. She says that she has a volunteer who is experienced in this area and she will give her my number. Can she have my details? I give my first name only. I am beginning to feel the need to protect myself. I want to keep my work and personal life separate. It feels like a repetition of the difficulties that I experienced when I was raped. I was a nurse, in need of medical attention but I didn't want the whole hospital to know! I remember that desperate feeling of wondering where I could go to remain anonymous. Now I am a counsellor, a parent mentor and a help-line co-ordinator wanting information. I'm angry that it has to be this difficult.

A few days after contacting Victim Support, I get a call from the manager saying that the volunteer has been trying to contact me but I keep cutting her off. I am astounded. I have been checking my phone, desperate for an appointment because I want the infor-mation before the police travel to interview the man who raped me this week.

The following day I get a call from the volunteer who again refers to the fact that I haven't answered her calls. What calls? Not the best start. We try to arrange to meet. The manager had suggested that I could come into the offices one evening. I suggest perhaps we could meet one evening this week but the volunteer is busy in the evenings, cooking dinner for the family. I remain polite and make conversation and say, "yes, it is busy, I have three children." I ask when she is available. As luck would have it, she runs a surgery session at the front of the hospital on a Tuesday morning. I am working for the Patients' Association helpline at the back of the hospital for two hours that morning and could pop along and meet her before going off to my afternoon job. I check where she wants to meet. I feel my heart sink when she says she will be at a desk in the corridor near the hospital main entrance. I have already said that I know a lot of people locally. She says there is a quieter place that we could go to. That's good!

Wednesday. Today is the day that the police travel to the north of England to interview the man who raped me. I wake with a cracking headache. I couldn't sleep. I woke up almost every hour and got up feeling exhausted. I remind myself of how I used to keep going when the children were babies. I have breakfast and shower and start my day. I don't want what's happening with my case to get in the way of what I'm doing now. One of the things I am doing is writing a case study for my counselling degree. The client I write about was raped on a cliff edge when she was 15.

Mid-morning, I leave work with five minutes to spare to go and meet the woman from Victim Support. Hopefully I will just make it in time. On the way up to the main entrance I meet a friend who is a midwife. We chat. She's stressed because of a complaint from a patient that might go to court. I nearly confide in her. I want to tell her that it is stressful having any part in an investigation. Then I notice we're almost at the front of the hospital. How can I shake her off? I don't want her to see me going to the Victim Support desk. She turns off just before I get there.

I meet the volunteer and she looks at an area in a corner with some seats but two old ladies are sitting there. Not to worry there is a room we can use. Sorry the room is already taken. Plan B. We can use the Patient Advice and Liaison office. I don't mind if the member of staff is present, do I? Sorry, yes, I do. I am meant to be setting up a meeting with them as part of my work on the helpline. Thankfully the member of staff offers to leave us alone and says we can close the blinds. The volunteer doesn't do this. I can be seen by everyone passing. By this point I don't care. Just let me ask my questions.

I find out that it is standard procedure for the defendant to be given the victim's name. As to having so many different police contacts, the volunteer has checked and this is the way Sapphire units are working at present. The Met police are cutting back, the budget is tight. Staff are on a ten-week rotation to the unit. Ok, so at least I know that this is what to expect. Then, onto the more important information.

What does an interview under caution mean? It means the police will caution the defendant at the start of their interview. It also means that this incident will be on his record for six years and if anyone reports something about him in the future the police will act on it immediately. After the interview today the police will spend about three weeks looking at the case and deciding if there is enough evidence to bring it forward to the Crown Prosecution Service. They have to be certain that there is because funds are tight and they chuck out a lot of cases even when there is DNA evidence. As this is a historical case it is unlikely that it will go anywhere. Different to the information I had from Bruce, the ex-police officer who encouraged me to report this. Also, in the remote chance of it going to court the volunteer informs me that they would 'rip me to shreds.' I'm angry at the unfairness. You know what, I would like to rip him to shreds. He ripped me apart when he raped me. He killed a part of me, stone dead. That youthful, foolish, fun loving, fancy-free part of me died that night.

If it does go to the CPS it will take about nine weeks for them to decide if they will drop the case or bring it to court. I'm looking at either three weeks or three months in total before I know the outcome. The other scenario the volunteer drops into the conversation is that he could plead guilty, 'you'd be surprised, some of them do'. So, what would happen then? He might get away with a fine and community service. I ask if she really thinks a consultant neuro- surgeon is going to do community service. Perhaps not, very unlikely that he will admit anything.

Tomorrow I'm going to get a call from an officer who I have spoken to once telling me how my rapist responded in the interview today. I know it will be difficult to hear whatever he says. It's nearly midnight. I've had just over half a bottle of wine before writing this. I hoped it might soften the edges, take away some of the pain I feel.

Chapter 8

October 2008

I got my phone call the next day. It's taken me three weeks before I could bring myself to write about this again. I was in the playground at 3.15 collecting my youngest daughter, Annie, from school. I asked if I could call back in a few minutes but was told that the officer wasn't on her usual number so needed to talk to me now. I go to the first quiet space that I can find, just outside the school gate where the mums with dogs usually stand. This is where I hear the news that the police are not going to take any further action.

They interviewed the man who raped me yesterday but do not have enough evidence to bring the case forward to the crown prosecution service. They say there is no medical evidence. What about the hospital discharge note that I've seen in my GP records stating that I needed stitching? That's not enough for the

CPS. The officer is sorry, she knows it's not the news that I want to hear. Has she had any training in breaking bad news to people? It would have helped if I could have met with her face to face and not heard this on the phone in the way that I did. In the middle of the call Annie comes to find me and I put my hand up for her to go away. I hope that my two beautiful, blond, trusting, innocent daughters never have to experience this. My wish is that no one should ever experience sexual violence but when they do I hope they are met with more understanding, compassionate support.

By the end of the year, once I have recovered from the ordeal of reporting to the police, I start to feel differently. I feel better for knowing that the man who raped me has been called to account for his actions. There may not have been enough evidence to proceed with the case but by reporting it to the police I was sending a strong message to him that what he did to me was wrong.

For the first time in many years, I feel like celebrating at New Year. I suggest to Pete that we open a bottle of champagne. I am deeply disappointed when he doesn't feel like celebrating with me. Sadly, this marks the start of a deterioration in our marriage. We've both worked so hard to care for our children and juggle work commitments that there hasn't been much time for us to nurture our relationship. It's not really surprising that our marriage starts to crumble.

Despite going to couple's counselling and then medi-
ation we separate eighteen months later.

Chapter 9

I often wonder about how many other people in the medical profession have been raped. We've heard so much more about sexual abuse in other areas since Operation Yewtree in 2012 which started with the investigation of Jimmy Savile and then went on to investigate other living people. Then there have been other organisations, the church, football, gymnastics, horse-racing. Hardly a month goes by without hearing about more abuse. Why haven't we heard about the medical profession? It is my belief that sexual violence is common amongst medical professionals but this is just my belief and I don't have any facts to back it up. I do have anecdotal evidence. I worked with a parent whose teenage daughter was self-harming. As a Parent Mentor I had just six sessions to help introduce positive parenting strategies to improve communication in the family. Listening is a key skill and I start by listening to the mother's story. At the time of meeting her she was in receipt of benefits and struggling to manage financially. Her story broke my heart.

This woman was a doctor. When she was first qualified and working as a junior doctor, she was raped by the Consultant whose team she was a part of. She fell pregnant as a result of the rape. She left the profession that she had trained for years for. She experienced poor mental health and wasn't able to work. In recent times she had confided in a neighbour who she thought was a friend. The neighbour went and told the daughter that she was conceived from rape and thus the self-harming began. How many more doctors abuse their position? The hierarchy sickens me to my core. I was a newly qualified staff nurse and so I was raped by a junior doctor. She was a junior doctor so she was raped by the Consultant.

Chapter 10

1987/2014

It sounds silly now but I wasn't able to name my experience as rape for a long time. I knew that I'd had this awful experience and I'd felt suicidal but because I let this man into my room, I took the blame for what happened. None of the medical professionals that I was seen by named it as rape.

Later in the year after it happened, I start dating someone called Thomas. He is a qualified psychiatric nurse and has moved from Ireland to do his general nurse conversion course. I really like him and feel safe with him. We start seeing lots of each other. I am nervous about any intimacy. He wants to know what has made me so unhappy. I am surprised that it shows so much and decide to confide in him. I tell him about my experience at New Year and how I ended up in hospital. He does something really important and he says 'Jenny, that was rape'. Still, I don't really take it in and I don't write the word 'rape' in my diary. Years later this conversation comes back to me. When I start talking in counselling it helps that Thomas had already named the experience for what it was.

When I am in my late forties, I meet up with Thomas again. I contact him through LinkedIn and he is coming to London for a conference. We go for a meal and fill each other in about the paths our lives have taken. He has been very successful and risen to the top of the nursing profession. He has four children and I have three. He has done lots of work around suicide prevention. Also, he has been involved in nurse training and been part of a programme teaching nurses how to respond to victims of sexual assault. I am so moved by this that I decide to take a risk and see if he remembers the conversation he had with me all those years ago. He takes a moment and then his eyes open wide and he says yes, he remembers. I explain how much it helped me that he had named my experience for what it was, rape. I am so thankful for this. He is genuinely pleased that his words had been helpful to me. I come away from meeting Thomas feeling as if something has shifted in me. Here is someone who knew me when I was 21 and was the first person who used the word rape. It feels like another layer of proof that it actually happened. As I write this, I feel sadness for the missed opportunity to name my experience when I turned up at hospital. If it had been named I may have been able to start healing from it sooner. Instead, it oozed its noxious poison into all areas of my life and it was sixteen years before I began to talk about it.

Chapter 11

2021, thirty five years after the rape

I'm scrolling through my emails absent mindedly when one of them grabs my attention. I am suddenly alert and interested in what it says. It is from a small organization that has a project working with victims of sexual violence and the media. I'd previously attended a writing workshop that was run by an author and it had been very good. This email is offering the opportunity of taking part in a Channel 4 debate about rape. The debate will come after an hour and a half long documentary that follows Avon and Somerset police as they investigate rape cases. The debate will have a panel and everyone in the audience will be a victim/survivor. I don't need to spend much time pondering this, I just know that I want to take part.

I email the organizer and she passes on my details to the Assistant Producer, Annie. Annie calls me and goes through some questions including when I was raped and when I reported it to the police. It's not easy talking to someone I have never met about something so personal but Annie has a warm manner and I am strangely reassured that she has the same name as my youngest daughter. We identify that one of the things I found really hard when I went through the process of reporting to the police was the fact that they prom- ised I would have a named officer but I ended up speaking to someone different almost every time they spoke to me with a query or update. Annie wants to know if I will have a question for the panel or if I will just be part of the audience. I think that I will remain quiet, it will be enough just being there. Is it those old feelings of shame that still keep me silent?

I speak to my daughters and son about the fact that I will be going on the programme. My daughter Annie has a strong reaction. She doesn't think it is a good idea. Some of it is because she is protective of me. She asks if I have thought about people who are only acquaintances seeing me on television. Do I really want everyone to know what my experience is? She goes on to say that it's not just about me. What if any of her friends see me on the programme? Shame runs deep and I am sad that Annie's generation continue to feel it. But isn't that exactly why we need to be making programmes like this and talking about rape? If we're not talking about it there is no hope of change.

I don't hear anything for a couple of weeks and just when I have more or less resigned myself to not going on the programme, I get a call from the producer Annie. They would like me to be part of the debate. It will be filmed on the following Saturday at studios in London. I know the area well; it is where my sister lives and I've walked past the studios hundreds of times. It feels like a good sign and it's reassuring to know where it is. Annie says she will email all the details the following week. It will take up most of the day. We will need to be Covid tested to start with and then we will watch the documentary. The debate will follow this. Days go on and still no email. Maybe there is a problem, maybe it won't go ahead after all. Finally on the Friday we get some information. Annie has been unwell with Covid and her colleague Georgia will be at the studios on the Saturday. It feels like another good sign, my daughter Annie's middle name is Georgia. I feel energized now that it's definitely going ahead.

I arrange to meet three other survivors from the organization who sent the original request out and also a member of staff who will be there to support us. We will meet at the station and walk to the studios together. I start to feel nervous on my way to the station. Do I really want to be on television? Maybe the camera won't focus on me. There is a trespasser on the railway track further up the line and my train is delayed. Suddenly I really want to get there and do this. We inch forward and then stop again. It feels like an agonizing wait. I message the others and let them know I will be running late. They are happy to wait for me and eventually I arrive and meet them. I have got to know one of the others quite well from a survivor's writing group which takes place over zoom. It's really nice to meet her in person. She says that I am taller than she imagined. I guess it's hard to tell when you've only seen someone's head on a screen!

We spend a long time waiting around after we have done our covid tests. A young woman who has come on her own joins our little group. She was raped when she was sixteen and in another country. She is now an activist and is trying to get things changed at her university in the way they handle sexual assault. I feel heavy. The sheer weight of the numbers of women who have been raped presses down on me. We watch the documentary for an hour and a half and it's not an easy watch. It is so difficult to get a prosecution in rape cases.

Finally, we go into the studio and it is not how I imagined it would be. Seats are arranged in small groups and a row around the edge. I'd imagined a tiered seating arrangement a bit like on Question Time. This feels more exposed. We don't get to choose where we sit, our names are on the seats. I sit in between two others. I have a moment where I wonder what would happen if I feel panicky and want to get out but it passes. Two women who featured in the documentary are also present and I think how brave they are. The panel is made up of a former chief of the crown prosecution service, a defence barrister and a police chief. No one from the CPS took up the offer to be on the panel. It's infuriating!

At the beginning of the debate the Chair asks everyone who has been raped to stand up. It is a powerful moment when everyone in the room stands up. People start asking their questions. The Chair is very good and she won't let the panel get away with wriggling out of questions. It feels as if the debate is going on for a long time. One woman becomes angry with a comment from the defence barrister. She says 'don't patronize me' and I wonder if this will be edited out or not. At the end of the debate the Chair asks for one final comment. A young woman puts her hand up, "Don't rape people!" She gets a round of applause.

On my way home I realise that I am incredibly tired. I feel heavy and drained. I phone my daughter, Rachel and ask her to order us a pizza. I am so glad to get back home and relax with her. A few days later and I am feeling better, better than I have felt for a long time.

By standing up and being counted I took another step towards letting go of the shame that I have carried for so long. The shame never belonged to me; it belongs to the perpetrator.

A couple of months later and I decide to watch the documentary again. The statistics that are cited in the programme are deeply depressing. I feel physically sick after watching it.

Fewer than 20% of victims report to the police.

Just over 1% of rapes both reported and unreported to the police end in a conviction.

Only 7% of rape cases reported to the police are referred on to the Crown Prosecution Service.

The average rape investigation takes more than two years from report to trial. Since the pandemic rape and serious sexual cases waiting more than a year to get to court have increased by more than 400%.

My heart is shattered. This is the reality of rape.

Acknowledgements

With thanks to Reverend Dermot O'Neill for his prayers when I was most in need of them.

Thank-you to Survivors Voices for all your support and for helping me to feel less alone.

https://survivorsvoices.org/

Other support
Rape Crisis - https://rapecrisis.org.uk

0808 500 2222

About the author

Jenny lives in London. She has 3 grown up children and is fostering a cat called Gigi. She worked as a nurse for 18 years and much of this time was spent as a District Nurse. Jenny went on to train in counselling and parenting work. She spent several years working with young families in South London. Currently Jenny has taken a break from work and thinks she may have accidentally retired.

About the designer

Artist Catherine E. Holbrook is a creative spirit based in the heart of Yorkshire where she plays piano, writes her own music and works on various creative community and education projects both online and in-person. Her work possesses a rare authenticity that touches the hearts and souls of those who encounter it.

You can find out more about Catherine's work by visiting her website: www.catherineholbrook.co.uk

Other projects that might be of particular interest to readers and Survivors are:

Catherine's blog 'An Artist's Response . . .' https://anartistsresponse.wordpress.com/ which includes her creative ponderings and responses to life, faith, the world and her own journey as a Survivor.

Catherine's music for solo piano **Barefoot Piano Prayers** https://barefootpianoprayers.bandcamp.com/

About Survivors Voices Press

Survivors Voices Press (SVP) is a survivor-led independent publisher that amplifies the voice and experience of survivors, promoting understanding of trauma and ally-ship with survivors of abuse.

Our mission is to provide a trauma-informed platform for survivors' work, filling the gap in mainstream publishing and challenging the stigma associated with accounts of abuse.

SVP is a project of Survivors Voices, a survivor-led organisation that turns the pain of abuse into the power to improve responses to trauma. We work with survivors of all types of abuse and are a non-profit organisation.

We run peer support groups, undertake research,

promote co-production and create change through education, activism and publications.

We work anywhere to engage and amplify the voice of survivors. If you are a survivor who needs support or wants to be heard, a practitioner who wants to listen, or an ally who wants to support us, we want to hear from you.

connect@survivorsvoices.org
www.survivorsvoices.org
X: @voiceofsurvivor
Facebook: survivorsvoicesuk
Instagram: survivors_voices

You are not alone

If the issues in this book have affected you or someone you know, you can find out about the help we offer and many other support organisations on our support page https://survivorsvoices.org/support/

www.ingramcontent.com/pod-product-compliance
Lightning Source LLC
Chambersburg PA
CBHW031401060726
47590CB00007B/2886